Balls
from the queue

"MATCH"

The 3rd of the trilogy
"GAME, SET & MATCH"
(Including a brief spell of rain)

Pavement Poetry 'caught' during Wimbledon 2010
In an unofficial one-man fringe event
www.poemcatcher.com

Inspiration on the fly
Published by PoemCatcher Creations
Salisbury Centre
2 Salisbury Road
Edinburgh, EH16 5AB

www.poemcatcher.com

Copyright
All the poems in this book were donated with love and permission to be published. Besides it would be thievery to steal the copyright from the authors themselves. It remains their own.
This is their beautiful creativity and I am just a creative collator.

The back page photo was taken in a daring, hi-tech photo shoot. Fortunately the stunt-double was only slightly injured. Sincere thanks to Jane Barlow for her photographic vision and expertise.

Design by Trevor at Fresh Digital

Use of this material is welcomed – providing it inspires, engages and enthrals audiences.
Each and every poem in this book is brilliant. If you disagree, send £10 with your complaint to a child in Haiti.

This is a 1st edition
It was produced in the last days of the queue at 2010

"MATCH"
ISBN 978-0-9566018-4-1

Be proud to own it!
Excellent toilet reading
Best before: 06/2011
Do not smash, volley or drop. Does not bounce.

For my Dad
Whose last words to me were

"practice what you love"

If you share his love of tennis or golf
You'll understand that
it takes 3 balls
to
practice what you love

About the Mess

Think, feel, doodle, make a list, ~~scratch some lines out~~, start again, find more paper, talk to your friends, gather ideas, just look around. They are here to be found.

Many of you did,
believed that you could
You did brilliant
I knew that you would
I love your first efforts
With edits and all
The edge of creation
A little bit raw.

P.S. this book is full of mistakes. Such is life.
Some are mine, some are yours.
I don't mind.
The struggle for perfectionism ain't worth the stress.
I far prefer a creative mess.

£2 per book goes to charity

SOS Children's Villages provides a family for life for children who have lost their parents through war, famine, disease, natural disaster and poverty. Over 78,000 orphaned and abandoned children are cared for by SOS mothers in clusters of family homes in more than 500 of our unique Children's Villages in 124 countries worldwide. Thousands more children benefit from SOS Children's outreach support which includes education, vocational training, medical care and community development programmes. SOS Children also provides emergency relief in situations of crisis and disaster, and continues to support families in earthquake and tsunami-affected countries.

Registered Charity Number 1069204
www.soschildrensvillages.org.uk

100-and-something pages of fresh poetry

*Nearly 150 co-authors
Sitting on the grass
Queuing
At Wimbledon 2010*

Contents

- CHAMPIONSHIP MUSINGS 12
  - Ace 12
  - 78 & 79 13
  - Roddick Lymerick 14
  - Waitrose High Juice 14
  - Wimbledon – The Championship 2010 15
  - 'n Gedig 16
  - Wimbledon's Great 16
  - Lady Luck 17
  - Unite 18
  - 40 – Love 19
  - The Tarttelin Set 20
  - The Tarttelin Set Continued 21
- RAIN STOPS PLAY 24
  - Wet Tent 25
- FOOD FIESTA 32
  - At Wimbledon Park 32
  - The Queue 33
  - Pei Bwthyn 34
  - (Pizza Box Poetry)Serve and Swallow 35
  - Pizza Poetry Express 36
  - Trailer Ode 37
- THE HONORARY STEWARDS 40

Sleeping for Tennis 40

Islands 41

He had his fill on Henman Hill 42

What's a queue card? 43

Speculation 44

Security 46

Left Luggage B V.1 47

Left Luggage A 48

QUEUE SPECIALS 52

A poem about a Queue 52

Wimbledon 53

From the big blue tent 54

Off we went 55

Queue Buddies 55

The HSBC Q 56

Wimbledon Waiting 57

The Queue 58

The Smith's Guide to Wimbledon Camping 59

What Wimbledon means to me 60

A Poem 61

From Finland 62

The Big Screen 63

A Dream Realized 64

Ode to Queuing 66

- Queue No. 32 67
- Me, you and the Queue 68
- Done 69
- The last shall be first 70
- The Long Wait for the men's Quarter-final 71
- 3.50 a.m. 72

MURRAY MANIA 76
- Tim's Limerick 76
- Peace Out 76
- English Love, Advantage Scotland 77
- In The Queue 78
- Tom and Abi's Wimbledon 80
- The Media v Murray 81
- Murray Meets his Match 81
- Barmy Army 82
- The Champion 83
- Wimballerm… 84
- Patient 85
- Dreams at SW19 87

FROM THE FINALS 90
- Bum Tweks 90
- Beginnings and Ends 91
- Tennis Match 92
- By J. E. KilleMatt Harvey 92

Matt Harvey 93
Ladies' Singles Final 95
Nicked 96
Wimbledon Men's Final 98
To the LTA 99
Your fresh poem about tennis goes here 100
Your fresh poem about this book goes here 101
IN CONCLUSION 102
A personal note about this project 102
Apologies (from you to me) 103

Championship Musings

CHAMPIONSHIP MUSINGS

Ace

Twack,
Skid,
Thud,
Applause.

By Mike Willis

78 & 79

On a glorious sunny day
Watching Federer and Nadal play
Camping in the overnight queue
Even having to use a portable loo!

Eating a punnet of strawberries and cream
All this excitement I think I might scream
At 100 mph the balls will be served
Some will fly straight, others will be curved.

Sometimes the ball will be hit just out
Leading the umpires and ballboys to shout
But hopefully Murray, the win he will snatch
In the final Game, Set and Match.

By Iain and becky

Roddick Lymerick

There was an American called Roddick
Who was a frightful alcoholic
After the first over
He had a terrible hangover
And then he realized he was supposed to be playing
                                              tennis and not cricket

By Harry Prosser

Waitrose High Juice

O Poet catcher
At cha leasure
How can we measure
Such a Scottish treasure

There's an element of menace
Collecting poems about tennis
What a premise!

By Norfolk & Chance

Wimbledon – The Championship 2010

A fortnight once a year
On the green lawns of Wimbledon all the fans cheer.
Come rain or shine, they line the queue,
Some passers by call them 'fou'.
Words no matter , we are here to stay,
Why else would we come for the play?
If you fight with tradition,
You'll be missin'
Thanks to the stewards,
They'll be fewer.
Through the large gates
We must wait
'till 10:00
It is when
Backs turn and fans will learn
Walk don't run or they'll be no fun.
Court 18 the fans will smile
It might be a while.
A five setter
The longest match ever.
Centre Court, it's the scene
Oh my lord, its the Queen.
Bottle of Pimms, Sorry to Tim
'Berries and Cream won't keep us lean
Roger the King
'Yes' he'll sing
After 14 days the trophy he'll raise
Never forget the experience I've had
No doubt about it, tomorrow I'm sad.

By Taylor Butch

'n Gedig

(Afrikaans)

Dis baie vroeg en ek is baie moeg
Die son kruip weg en die koffie is lekker
Ons sit hier op on kombersies en dink aan
Allerhande rymende versies

Deur Emma Tromp & Elmier Taljaard

Vreeslike baie dankie vir hierdie gedig. Ek woon in Edinburgh en het lank laas Afrikaans gepraat. Ek waardeur dit baie.

Wimbledon's Great

Grass green
Skies Blue
Queue Long
The tennis ball goes bong, bong, bong.

By Leah and Evin

Lady Luck

I got up a at four
And walked out the door,
Heading down the street
it was very quiet,
not even a bird's tweet.
Onto the tube and Southfield station,
Still not much activity nor animation.
But then left at gate 10
and into the green
And there were hundreds of people
equally as keen
Lady luck was on my side
And ticket 497 she gave
That gets me on centre court
- So fantastic   –
I better behave.

By Matthew Press

Unite
_____

Look upon the moon and know
That wherever you are you're not alone
Like in the field at Wimbledon
Where tennis and tents unite us all

By Tricia Gadd

40 – Love

40 - Love

Tennis is a love game,
no match is ever the same.
It makes you work hard,
and feel your every body part.
The directions you choose,
will decide whether you win or lose.
But winning or losing, it doesn't Really matter,
it's all about the playing together. ☺

By Felice Luijten

The Tarttelin Set

      A cat I saw
          On Wimbledon Green
      "Meow" he said
         And so did I.

By Tom Tarttelin

    Green Green
    I'm green at queuing here
    Blue Blue
    I'm blue from quehing here
    Yellow Yellow
    I'm too yellow in the night-queue here
    Blue, Green, Yellow
    Showing my colours at Wimbledon Park

By Pat Tartelin

The Tarttelin Set Continued

Hennessey and Chemistry
With Dennis Kwee in Tennessee
Was to much for me
So I thought I'd see
If Benzadrine and Kerosene
Could get me in to the tennis ... Eeee.

By Abigal Tarttelin

A poem I've been told to write,
Though we've been camping all night
Too tired to think,
And in need of a drink
And still no tennis in sight

By Tammy Lai

RAIN

RAIN STOPS PLAY

It did rain this year at Wimbledon. I promise.
There was an intense shower one morning around 8 am. And although it had absolutely no impact on the tennis, those of us waiting in the queue had a few words to say about it

Wet Tent

Cabin-ed in a tent of rain
Trying to stay dry
But all that trying trying does
Is the obvious deny.
There's wetness here
No doubt at all
We're likely damp tonight
The tennis, all will be delayed
The camp's a muddy sight.

For 8 days now we've seen the sun
    And gathered poems of glee
And now its time for poems of rain
    And tennis misery.

I would head out
to collect some poems
but I'm rather poor equipped.
This borrowed tent
Is home for now
Till this passing shower
Is nipped.
I wonder how much longer,
How much longer I'll be here
I wonder if I'll make it dry
 To my house of warmth, so dear
And I wonder if its worth it
To try to write this book
When I'm trapped inside a tent
Kilted in a nook

So I write because I can
There's a luxury of time
When the weather's foul at Wimbledon
And you're waiting in the line.
I hear the pitter patter
Of the raindrops on the tent
And think about the tennis
And this blessing, heaven sent.

And I'd like to buy a brolley
To make it to the loo.
They're awfully, awfully far away
From the rainy queue.

"Protect the poems" is my first thought
They're no good when they're damp
So quickly filed within my bag
Avoid the drip of pen and stamp.

And still it rains
   And still it rains
      I hear the every drop
         Its been a whole ten minutes
           And I wonder if it'll stop
Already seems eternity
  Trapped inside this tent
    Hearing voices outside
      Braving heaven's vent.

Oh, drama from the tournament
  As dreams get washed away
    'Cept for Centre's roof of course
      That lets continued play.

Tennis is the sport of kings
In fact a sport for all
We learn it when we're children
When we cannot hit the ball.
There's tennis-set, the training ground
For little kids at school
And beach-bats for on holiday
A useful training tool

As summer comes to season
The French and Queens come by
Clay and grass a different class
A grandslam win to try

We all have our favourites
The Champions of our hearts
We love to cheer the underdogs
Who challenge from the start.

We grow to love new faces
As our favourites tire with age
And then we change allegiance
New youngsters all the rage.
Thinking fondly of the past
The fashions that went by
The players and spectators
All trying to look fly

Big branding's now the business
The players paid to be
Dressed in something fancy
And sponsored by Nike.

The etiquette for camping
Is governed by "The Rules"
No barbeques or corkscrews
Or other dangerous tools.

One bottle is the limit
Per person, that's enough
To get the party started
And end before its rough

The mornings in the campsite
Are brisk and full of cheer
Newcomers off the early trains
And Aussies drinking beer.

The Saffa's they are here as well
The Kiwi's jump the Q
The French, The Yanks & Poms of course
All wait without ta-do.

This year there is a poet
Adorning centre court
He's writing about tennis
As we guess he ought

There's also a poem-catcher
Kilted with a net
Wandering the Q's for poems
For a trilogy poem set.

By PoemCatcher

Written in one deep breath
In the only rain shower of
Wimbledon 2010

Food Fiesta

FOOD FIESTA

At Wimbledon Park

Ducks
Their beady eyes
They eye up my pies
While they fly by.
And I say bye
I never want to see you near my pies

By Smartie Martie

The Queue

How can there be so many like-minded folk?
Who queued through the night or early awoke?
However jealous I am of the early queue cards
A day at Wimbledon beats the pain by yards

Offers of takeaways come from every direction
The night one takes clever selection

Frisbee and football or a game of catch
Are all fun but there is only one form of match
That everyone here is waiting to witness
The skill, the drive and incredible fitness
Tennis is the reason for which we are queuing
I cannot wait for tomorrow for a day of viewing.

By Laura Lambert

Pei Bwthyn

Pei Bwthyn

Bore Da, Gallai i cael pei bwthyn?

Wyt ti moen sglodion?

Na, dim sglodion diolch

Iawn, mwynhewch!!"

By M.U.R.R.A.Y.

(Pizza Box Poetry) Serve and Swallow

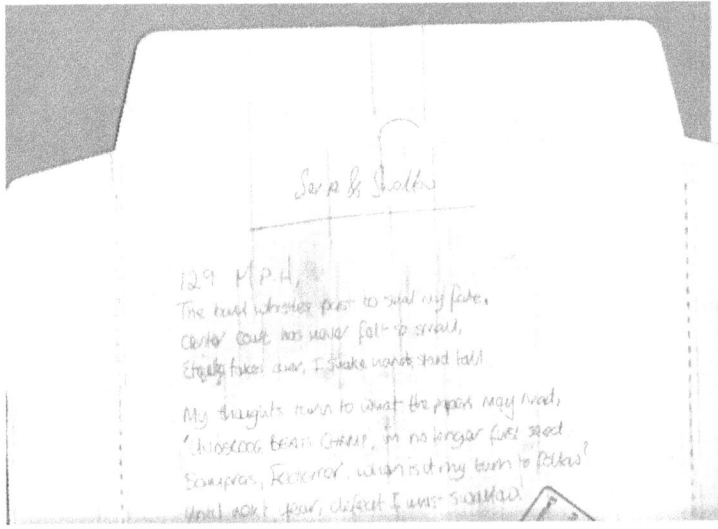

129 M.P.H.
The balls whistles past to seal my fate.
Centre Court has never felt so small,
Etiquette takes over, I shake hands, stand tall.

My thoughts turn to what the papers may read
"UNDERDOG BEATS CHAMP", I'm no longer first seed.
Sampras, Federer, when is it my turn to follow?
Until next year, defeat I must swallow!

By David Warren

Pizza Poetry Express

Cheese and tomato
Anchovies and ham
I'm a tennis fan.

By Chris Hurley
Elotributeband.com

Trailer Ode

To Wimbledon we do come to sell,
It's our idea of a working hell.
Burgers, sausages and bacon too,
We cook them all to the endless queue
They queue and camp in organized rows
With sun umbrellas and skimpy clothes
All in hope, but some in doubt
Of whether they can watch
From Murray Mount

By Terri McDonough

A special repeat poem from "SET"

The Honorary Stewards

THE HONORARY STEWARDS

This section is for the stewards and staff who volunteer or work at Wimbledon. Thank you for your commitment to creating this great event.

Sleeping for Tennis

Up all night
What a sight

Lost wallets found
On the ground

Wake up at five
You must feel alive

If you come to watch Murray
You must hurry

Moon turns to sun
Lets have some fun

By Jess, Elie & Becca

Islands

Bathgate road,

I knew you in a roundabout way

By StewardsRus

He had his fill on Henman Hill

There was a young man called Dennis
Who came to Wimbledon to watch the tennis
He went on to Henman Hill
And of Pimms he had his fill
And got ejected from the ground as a menace

By Robert Burns
A.K.A an anonymous steward

What's a queue card?

When the queue is long and unending
And thousands are struggling with tents
When the queue cards are unknown and pending
Whom will you turn to to vent?

Will it be the innocent day steward
Who's been polite and patient for hours?
Who's organized thousands into "k-lines"
And stacked brochures tower upon tower.

Well if this is your choice dear camper,
Of course we are here to help,
But don't be surprised if your steward is tired
And isn't able to answer your yelp.

In all my advice would be
To speak to your steward with glee
Be smiley and kind,
Though still speak your mind
(failing that, just buy them an ice cream)

By Phoebe Dickinson

Speculation

(Read with over-the-top melancholy, romanticism and blues)

I imagine
So very many things
I imagine

You see, your beauty,… has inspired me
My visits with you …every single day
They've been a joy …when all around was bleak
Brought me happiness…Your glowing sunshine ray

I imagine if I asked you out to dinner
Imagine you dining out with me
Imagine you're delicious
To kiss and cuddle;
Snuggle – ly.

I imagine I might ask you to my tent
Imagine of the night I'll spend with you
Imagine all the little pleasures
That keep me warm the whole night through.

I imagine you're too pretty to say yes
To my imaginary invites real or dreamed
Imagine your corporate finance boyfriend
Earns more than I or even than the Queen

The hope that lives alive in my imagination
I've left it there for no-one else to see.
I'll quietly go about my business
Never dare to live the dream I dream.

*There were many promotions teams working the queue.
This poem is inspired by one of the gorgeous promotional
girls who caught a few hearts in her photo-booth.
For privacy reasons I can't say who.*

Dedicated to the men at Left Luggage A

Security

Left Lugguage B is the name of our crew
Protecting the public is what we do
Guarding, touting, checking and searching
All at G4S are very hard working

On the golf course & in the sun
We laugh with the fans & have lots of fun
But we never fail to protect the lives
Of children, husbands, grannies and wives

As the championships come to an end
We all bid farewell to our colleagues and friends
We will see you again in 2011
You'll find us at Apache at a quarter to 7.

By Natasha, Steph, Liz and Gen

Left Luggage B V.1

Sitting in the Wimbledon sun,
The security Guards are having fun

Constantly vigilant against the dangers
Of lock-knives, pepperspray and weirdo strangers

They're the envy of all with their immaculate tans
And the queuing public are their number one fans

Working real hard protecting the crowd
Hearing them cheer and shouting out loud!

By Saad, Jay & Leanne

Left Luggage A

Bring forth the bags,
The luggage that you leave
The friendly staff, with open arms
Your luggage they'll retrieve

I met the PoemCatcher
The highlight of the day
The weather may be wayward
But the poems never go astray

Here at left luggage
There's joy, cheer and fun
You'll see us in our cabins
Here at Wimbledon

By Marky Rich

Queue Specials

QUEUE SPECIALS

A poem about a Queue

Is there a q in racquet?
There is a queue in Wimbledon
And I am in the queue.
There is a q in queen and
There was a Queen at Wimbledon.
I queued in the queue to
Watch Sam Querry play.
Sam Querry won the Queen's
tournament. There are many
Q's in tennis, but one big
 queue at Wimbledon and I am in it.

By Mairi Clarke

Wimbledon

Where queuing queues queue
In the shape of a snake
At the pace of a snail

Where the stellar white stars
Are served by stewards
with more uniforms
than a military parade

By Shauna Mahlo Craxton

From the big blue tent

So where to begin,
Queue for a day and a half to get in,
"Is it really worth it?" you may wonder,
"OF Course" – even with England's rain and thunder
Some go for the atmosphere & the Pimms,
But we go for the great tennis even if its not Tim's,
Whilst Federer does a serve, lob and slice,
Nadal battles on to win it twice
Sitting on Centre Court admiring the view,
Thanking God we're not in that queue,
Munching on strawberries and cream,
In the distance hearing Sharapova scream,
Enjoying Centre Court and our favourite sport.

By Mark Potton, Lydia Fernandes and Zoe Weekes

Off we went

Off to Wimbledon we went

With our rucksacks and our tent

The weather's been mixed

But we'll see Fed's tricks

All in All, three days well spent

By Emma and Elisabeth

Queue Buddies

It started with a cider early
The approached by a man
Whose hair was curly
It'll move on to strawberries and cream
Whilst watching players
Smash out their dream.
At Pimm's O'clock
The balls will drop
And we'll all go stumbling home.

By Kelly, Annabel, Tish Corinne and Andrew

The HSBC Q

Red rope
Steel post x 11
Paint Brushes
Rollers
Eye bolts x 44
Screw-in eyes x 4
Silver van
White paint
3 bodies
1 narrator
1 honorary stewards (in the shade)

Perfecting the HSBC experience (day 8)

By PJ, Shaggy and Crabman

Wimbledon Waiting

They wait in couples
With cups of Pimms
And punnets of fruit
With aunties and uncles
Still disgruntled
from lack of sleep
and unexpected heat.
They chill... in the warmth
Meanwhile our army of ambushing smilers attack,
Pleading with sunners to take a pack
Of toothpaste or plasters
They'll be confiscated after
As I melt into grass
And the queues roll past
Crawling closer to courts.

By Ava Riby- Williams

On behalf of the toothpaste
and plasters promotional team
and their cheesy smiles.

The Queue

Waiting, waiting all night long
For the time,
The time to rise,
The early morning call
Will there be rain?
Or will the sun shine?
Will Federer triumph?
Will Nadal fall?
The long queue,
The Pimms,
The strawberries and cream,
Huge crowds,
Television screens
Henman Hill,
Exorbitant prices
Dejected screams:
Without these there'd be no Wimbledon feel!
Massive cheers resound of "What a great shot!"
But it's time for a break;
Its Pimm's O'clock!

By Robyn Margetto and Patrick O'Boyle

The Smith's Guide to Wimbledon Camping

If you have decided to come and camp for Wimbledon Tennis, there area few things that you need to do:

1. You need to book at least 2 days off work.
   You will need to get to the queue as quickly as you can. The sooner you arrive, the more chance you have of getting a ticket for Centre Court.

2. Makes sure you have the correct supplies.
   A tent is an essential requirement. The tent not only keeps you dry in the rainy weather, it also keeps you cool from the sun. you will need food, water, an umbrella, a sleeping bag or blanket and sunscreen.

3. Make sure to make friends with those ahead and behind you in the line. You may need to leave your tent for a quick trip to the ice-cream-man and having a friend in the line will keep your place for you.

4. You have to have a ball.
   What other time in sporting history are you able to camp for free? Make sure to take lots of photos and be kind to the stewards. (and no, they aren't all named 'Steward', that is their profession!)

5. Lastly, go and get some strawberries & cream to enjoy while you watch a game or two.

By Lyndall & heather Smith

What Wimbledon means to me

Wimbledon Park has

Incredible facilities that

Makes our camping experience

Brilliant and exciting

Leading to an

Enjoyable

Day

Of

Nothing but TENNIS

By Lyndall and Heather Smith

A Poem

Waking up at the crack of dawn
I rub my eyes, stretch and yawn
And suddenly excitement shone
As it's the morning of Wimbledon.
Among the people there is no menace
We're all here to watch some tennis,
We all know the terminator
Can be the one and only Federer
Australia is far from here,
But today I will shed no tear
Because the day will be so full of fun
Here, at Wimbledon.

By Sharea Jaijee

From Finland

Flying from Finland
To join this long queue
Sitting in line with
Not much to do
Sipping black coffee
And holding the queue card
Coveting centre court tickets
Quite hard

By Linda and Mika

The Big Screen

Give us a big screen,
Not strawberries and cream,
Whilst we're sitting out here in the sun.
We've been here two nights
We've had a few fights
But the worst thing is
I can't feel my bum
Yes there's conversation a'plenty
Friendly faces all around
But it's tennis we want
Another Murray Mound.
So give us our screen
I need tennis, I could scream!
Here in the queue at good ol' Wimbledon

By Dominic Himsworth

A Dream Realized

Arriving at Southfields,
We know what to do,
Walk down to Wimbledon,
And get in the queue.

Put up the tent,
Get out of the sun,
Crack open the drink,
And meet everyone.

Fast food and takeaway,
Poets with nets,
This whole experience
Is as good as it gets.

Now the sun sets,
We wait for Tuesday,
I can't wait to see,
The ladies at play.

Pimms in a glass,
Strawberries and cream,
But for so long,
Its all been a dream

Tomorrow that changes,
At Centre Court I will sit
Double faults and aces,
Attacks at the net.

There is no better
Way to have fun,
Than spending the day,
At the Great Wimbledon

By Ryan Griffith

Ode to Queuing

When playing Risk
Tom got quite pissed
To find that he was losing
He took the time
To make the rhyme
For to win at Wimbledon
Would be sublime.

By Tom

Queue No. 32

Wimbledon South-West London SW19
Home of British Tennis
So what does that mean?

A fortnight of tennis, drama and fun
This year little rain, soaring temperatures
And a whole lot of sun.

2 days in the queue,
To watch the men's quarters
Cheering on Fed with Myrka and daughters

Tsonga V Murray – we're in for a treat
Soderling V Nadal – he's the one to beat

Djokovic V Lu rounds things up for the men
As we quickly approach the Finals
Of Wimbledon 2010.

By Anthony Josephson

Me, you and the Queue

Me, You and the Queue

There were 4 girls who went off to the tennis
They soon discovered the queue was a menace
But when they finally got in
They watched all their favourite players win
And they went home full of hapiness.

By Hannah, Rebecca and Ruth

Done

Last Orange Wristband
Done.

Rachel was the last person in the queue to get a centre court access wristband

The last shall be first

The last shall be first and the first shall be last
Dark skies call the end
Lines that waited through the night
Summers waxing call

By Sebastian Roberts

*The first person to **not** get a centre court wristband on the last day of queue tickets*

The Long Wait for the men's Quarter-final

Grey tinged clouds drift by
Bright sunshine bulldozes through
Twelve spots of rain fall
On the psychology questionnaire
Two footballs
Are thumped
Three coloured pins juggled
A rounder is run
A gentle hum of contentment
Is the Wimbledon queue

By Maggie Wright

3.50 a.m.

3.50 a.m.
Out on the turps drinking Pimms
Got a call from the crew
That we were in.

On the N1 bus through Deptford we travelled
The sights of London's
Working class unraveled

At Waterloo we did run
And make the J-12,
This was going to be fun

Coffee and croissants, black cab, the queue
500 people in front
Surely we'll get through.

Wimbledon is where its at
Sunscreen, Pimms and
A Broad rimmed hat.

By Sue Noble, Michel Toohey & Amanda Flynn

Murray Mania

MURRAY MANIA

Tim's Limerick

There once was a player called Murray
Who played every game in a hurry
He worked and he toiled
We watched and we boiled
Till he beat Roger Fed with a flurry

By Tim Clarke

Peace Out

One day I went to Wimbledon
I bumped into a Scottishman
We got wasted at night
Stayed up till daylight

We had a banging time
Queuing in line
Waiting for Murray to shine

Peace Out

By Rachel Love, Carl Annie and Ray

English Love, Advantage Scotland

Here on the back of a world cup defeat
We all prey Murray serves us up a treat
Hundreds if Brits queue all night and all day
Knowing that tennis has Hawk-eye replay

Now let 2010 be our year
Where a Scotsman wins without any fear
So bring on tomorrow when the tides will turn
Or go home empty hands with only sunburn.

By Alex Beeton

In The Queue

British tennis at Wimbledon
Can often cause pain,
Many highs and lows,
But worst of all is the rain.
Inclement weather
is the last thing we need
dry sunny conditions will
see us Brits succeed.

Enthusiasts of all creeds
Travel from far and wide,
They camp, queue and jostle
To sit side by side.
There's two special sisters
Whose task every year
Is to embrace Wimbledon's gala
To shout, clap and cheer.

For Wongy and Mitchy
It's the only place to be,
Even vacating their homes
In Norfolk by the sea.
Come hell or high water,
The two weeks are a must
To endure the thrills of net calls
Chalk lines and dust.

They've seen Henman Rusedski
And other Brits strut their stuff,
But its ended the same
Just not quite enough.
But this year lloks good,
Our man's in a hurry
It's time to stand up
And be counted Mr Murray

By Susanne Pyefinch &Michele Jennings

Tom and Abi's Wimbledon

Would you camp for a ticket?

I Would...

Me too!

Because Wimbledon makes me happy

Like a winning Murray

Each hour's different

Do it!

Own it!

Now!

By Tom and Abi

The Media v Murray

The media, they hiped him up,
As only they can do.
But oor Andy was keel-hauled,
And Rafael went through.

Sander Crozier

Murray Meets his Match

There was a young player called Murray
Who on all his sets in a hurry
Until he met Rafa
That great Spanish gaffer
Who is hotter than Vindaloo Curry

By Goldfinger

Barmy Army

The Corby Bravehearts

The Champion

Murray is Mint
Venus is on a different planet
Tim used to cry 'Come on lets 'ave it'

Wimbledon is great
Spectators are having a ball in the sun
Some will queue overnight
Just to get in on the fun.

And when it is done
The people will leave
and the rubbish gone
All that remains is the achievement
Of a champion.

By Nick Thompson

Wimballerm…

We're at Wimbledon

In the queue

Making Conversation

Before we go through

Laughing and joking

Enjoying the sun

Dan, Matt, Hope & Katie

Only want to have fun

Now bring on a Murray victory

By Katie, Hope, Shim and Matt

Patient

Supported Andy all the way

He's improving every year,

But Raffa's on his game okay

Scotland waits again I fear.

By Ellen Hughes

Dreams at SW19.

Overnight campers in their vast array,
A plethora of tent colours; green, blue and grey.
Strawberries + cream, pimms + champagne
All the spectators pray for no rain.
The All England Club and their all white attire,
Hoping no players will have to retire.
Dreams for a British winner on Henman Hill,
the dream for Andy Murray lives on still.
Expectation, hope — a never-ending dream,
Maybe a new champion at SW19?

Dreams at SW19

Overnight campers in their vast array,
A plethora of tent colours; green blue and grey
Strawberries and cream, Pimms and champagne
All the spectators pray for no rain.

The All England Club and their all white attire,
Hoping no players will have to retire.
Dreams for a British winner on Henman hill,
The dream for Andy Murray lives on still
Expectation, hope – a neverending dream,
Maybe a new champion at SW19.

By Danielle Eales

From The Finals

FROM THE FINALS

Bum Tweks

Sitting here at Wimbers
With Nadal about to play
The way he tweks his bottom
Takes my breath away.

By Sheila Thain. Lybster

Beginnings and Ends

the finals came

with proud and fame

one person leaves the other stays

the time full of games

excitement and pace

it's coming to end

bringing fresh start

new passion and strength

..beginnings and ends

lovely romance

By A.E.G.

Tennis Match

Dong. First serve.

Bing bong
Bing bong. Baseline

Ping pong
Ping pong. Volley

Ding dong. Longest match ever.

Championship point.
King Kong!

It's not over yet:
Ying yang
Ying yang. Mixed doubles

By J. E. Kille

Matt Harvey

Ladies' Singles Final

it's Serena versus Vera
versus Vera Zvonareva
at the outset honours even
there could even be an upset
Vera's nearer than a lot get

Vera won't just play Serena
but Serena's mighty aura
this can make Serena meaner
or seem meaner, that's why Vera
's really got to go for shots that
she knows that she might not get yet
it's her best bet – take the battle
to Serena, and unsettle
her opponent, grasp the nettle

might Serena William's waver
in the face of Zvonareva?
or might Vera wilt and falter
as Serena's serves assault her
will Serena be in clover
and roll Zvonareva over
or conversely might Vera
take Serena to the cleaners?

well, with Elena Vesnina
she beat Venus and Serena
in the Ladies' Doubles quarters
so Serena really oughta
fear a Vera Zvonareva
upset – she knows she could not get
a more ominous opponent
which of them will seize the moment

Williams versus Zvonareva
honours even – all to play for

Ladies' Singles Final

Matt Harvey was Wimbledon's official "Poet in Residence." He graced Centre Court with a poem a day and offered many great reflections on Wimbledon in his numerous poems and press interviews.

Nicked

On my way to meet the bard,
 the one who has the stamp
Officialdom and title bear
The opening of the gates to him
To sit where other poets dare
To dream of place and pomp and Pimms.

When there with promptness, I inspired
A while around the gate 5 stile
The stewards from G4S with poems
They laughed a lot (and smiled)

'Till long came gallant officer,
A trite and pompous chap
To ask "what is your purpose here?"
You've been a long while near
The entrance to this courtside road
I think you're dodgy and must be towed
Away from here,

    Unsaid:
    "I'd like to catch a bloke
    Doing something wrong so folk
    will think I'm a talent
    to my profession
    of teaching other folk lessons

The bullying tactic, well it worked
My humour gone, my power shirked,
He nicked it as he took my name
Ignored my life, my quest, my gain.
He bullied in his faceless mask
He ignored me whole to do his task
An act of distance and demeanour
To establish rank, and power seena
As the one to be obeyed
The larky copper could not be swayed
That I, in fact, a meeting had,
"With the official poet", I bragged.

He offered squint a gaze to me
Requesting some identity
And proof, like such a thing exists
That this 'meeting' was no tryst.

My knees of jelly, this bully made
He pissed all over my parade,
Fair to say my boots were big
With 300 poems from this gig
And fair to say, I'd asked the steward
To slip me in (the copper knew it)

By PoemCatcher

A true story

Wimbledon Men's Final

The sun shines down on Wimbledon it is the last and final day;
The umpire sitting in his chair calls Berdytch to serve and play,
Centre Court mens final day and now has come the hour;
Nadal and Berdytch accross the net matching power with power.
At the peak of fitness, sweat on their brow, concentration on their faces;
Backhands, forehands booming serves each winning their share of aces.
Berdytch plays his very best running and chasing everything;
Nadal plays like a maestro you can hear his raquet sing.
Berdytch tried his utmost but no matter the stroke he played;
Nadal's raquet flashed through the air like Zorro's trusty blade.
The spectators cheered and applauded I,m sure they would concur;
With such ferocity he returned the ball at times it was a blur.
Once more Nadals forehand stroke turned defence into attack;
Berdytch put his shot out of court Nadal lay prone upon his back.
The match drew to its conclusion the crowd cheered on Henman Hill;
Nadal the tennis genius had won three straight sets to nil.
The Golden cup held aloft the crowd chanting his name,
Another Slam another title another chapter too his fame!!!

By Alan Wicksted

To the LTA

I, the tennis ball, would like to complain
About the hardships I suffer,
The abuse and the pain

I came out of the factory
All fluffy and yellow
Expecting a life
That was peaceful and mellow

Now Wimbledon's here,
I've had my ten minutes of fame.

I won't be back next year,
I've been discarded with shame.

Woefully yours

Bounceless

*A small petition was raised
on behalf of tennis balls rights.
It is hoped that the LTA will
Acknowledge this injustice
And respond with appropriate kindness
and compensation*

By Taraash and Stacey

Your fresh poem about tennis goes here

Your fresh poem about this book goes here

IN CONCLUSION

A personal note about this project

In my therapy practice, I spend time helping people find their vitality; the places in their lives that bring them pleasure and step them towards health.

> **Creative places are always wrapped in pleasure, its simply divine.**

This poem-catching project has all the ingredients of every dream.

> *The idea; the growing internal detail; the doubt; the fear; the uncertainty; the courage; the trust; the action; the leap of faith; the realisations of the obvious; the moments of sheer stupidity; the 'aha' moments; the perfectly unplanned change of direction; the trashy bits; the lost and found; the success ; the reflection and reward of completion.*

So does each and every poem in this book.

It has been a privilege to watch you write, create and journey through your 'creative ingredients' on a pavement and a park bench.

I have one wish...

> **Please Believe.**
> **Believe in yourself.**
> **Believe in your creativity.**   ***Its beautiful.***

Apologies (from you to me)

Dear PoemCatcher

Sorry for the handwriting that you could not read, and sorry for the metric rhythm that you could not follow and sorry for not giving the poem a title, and thank you, so much for giving it a title for me (why didn't you just ask?, I would have done it happily) and I forgive you for typing up the most poignant moment of the poem with the wrong word. (I promise to write neater next time).

Oh, don't worry about the auto-capitalising of all the little-letters I so carefully choose to punctuate. I understand the nuances of word-processing in a hurry.

Lastly sorry for not seeing my own brilliance. I wrote a great poem and then dissed it myself. I've had time to reflect and I'm pretty chuffed that I could write such an amazing poem so spontaneously. I really like my own poem. I was brilliant.

I promise to write some more

With Love
The Aspirational Poet

The End

This completes "MATCH" the third of the trilogy

BALLS from the queue
Game, Set and Match

Thank you.
PoemCatcher

www.ingramcontent.com/pod-product-compliance
Lightning Source LLC
Chambersburg PA
CBHW051455290426
44109CB00016B/1763